Location Analytics for Business

Location Analytics for Business

The Research and Marketing Strategic Advantage

David Z. Beitz

BEP BUSINESS EXPERT PRESS

First published in 2018 by
Business Expert Press, LLC
222 East 46th Street, New York, NY 10017
www.businessexpertpress.com

ISBN-13: 978-1-63157-142-8 (paperback)
ISBN-13: 978-1-63157-143-5 (e-book)

Business Expert Press Big Data and Business Analytics Collection

Collection ISSN: 2333-6749 (print)
Collection ISSN: 2333-6757 (electronic)

Cover and interior design by Exeter Premedia Services Private Ltd., Chennai, India

First edition: 2018

10 9 8 7 6 5 4 3 2 1

Printed in the United States of America.

Abstract

It's estimated that 80 percent of an organization's data contains spatial attributes, but many don't understand how to unlock the potential of this data for their organizations to make better decisions. You have just been handed the keys by finding this book.

Readers will unlock these methods by learning about location analytics as well as taking a deep dive into the Planned Grocery® platform created in part by the author. The Planned Grocery® location analytics platform has been mentioned in the Wall Street Journal, Forbes, Bloomberg, and Business Insider. A sampling of clients of Planned Grocery® include: Philips Edison and Company, Just Fresh, Slate Retail REIT, Wegmans, and Whole Foods.

The practical information in this book is designed to prepare you to recognize and take advantage of situations where you and your organization can become more successful using location analytics. This will be accomplished by taking you through an explanation of the fundamentals of location analytics, by looking at various case studies, by learning how to identify and analyze spatial data sets, and by learning about the companies that are doing interesting work in this space.

Keywords

data science, demographics, enterprise, Esri, GIS, location analytics, opportunity surface, planned grocery, predictive location analytics, real estate, site selection

Contents

Preface

My fascination with location analytics started in 1993 when I was an undergraduate at the University of South Carolina majoring in Geology. I attended an interpretation of aerial photos class, that I loved, and it was in that class that I discovered Geographic Information Systems (GIS). I had already changed majors several times so at this point I decided that I would get a cognate in Geography. At the time a cognate was almost like a second major, and this would allow me to fit in some GIS classes while still graduating almost on time. My geology professor Dr. John Shervais also allowed me to do an independent study using Esri (Environmental Systems Research Institute) ArcInfo GIS software to create a geologic map. Only problem with this project was that I didn't know EsriArcInfo or how to operate the UNIX workstation it was on. Dr. Shervais pointed me to the workstation and to the wall of literally 30 thick ArcInfo Manuals and said "Here it is, get started!" I spent many hours learning to navigate the UNIX operating system as well as learning Esri's ArcInfo software so that I could replicate an existing paper geologic map in to GIS. Even though it was a rather torturous experience, I came out with a real appreciation for GIS and what it could potentially do. At the end of the project I could not find an export or print command, so I had to take a picture of the computer screen as proof that I completed the project.

From there I got an internship at Wilbur Smith and Associates (now CDM Smith), a transportation planning firm, where I got to use GIS in several interesting ways. Sometimes I was making maps for exhibits on projects, other times we used GIS to create traffic analysis zones that were used in transportation planning software. This software would then show the roads that needed to be widened as population growth increased traffic on the road network. Back then working with census data was interesting because we had to go to a special library at the University of South Carolina to check out the CDs with the data we needed. Then we had to go through a lot of work to format the data in the way we needed it for use in the software. After I graduated, the firm hired me full time and I stayed there for about four years.

Then one day I noticed an ad where a local commercial real estate company was looking for a GIS and Research person. This company, called Edens and Avant at the time, focused on shopping centers and real estate brokerage. So, I took the job and started the GIS and Research program. I was the first person there doing computer mapping and was proud to do the first portfolio map showing the locations of their shopping centers. This was a great fit for many years. The company grew to be a significant player in the shopping center industry and I got to do a lot of interesting things with GIS and spatial data. During my tenure there we won Special Achievement Awards from Esri in 2001 and in 2012,[1] and I got to travel to most of the major cities on the east coast doing market analysis. The company paid for me to earn the LEED Green Associate designation from the U.S. Green Building Council. I also got involved with the Urban Land Institute by earning their Real Estate Development Certificate which required various classes in Century City, CA and Washington, DC.

One data set that I got to work with while I was there at the shopping center company, was provided by a company called SNL Real Estate, later acquired by S&P Global. The company that I was working for had a subscription to their data. S&P Global has amazing data that is used by leading investment banks, investment managers, corporate executives, ratings agencies, government agencies, consulting firms, law firms and media companies such as The New York Times, The Wall Street Journal, USA Today, Washington Post, Forbes and Fortune.[2] At the time I was a part of a two person GIS team and we were working on a location analytics project to better locate and analyze shopping center data. For example, using the right GIS software with this data set you can map out and study the demographics of all the locations of the major shopping center Real Estate Investment Trusts (REITs). The records for each shopping center had a longitude and latitude so we were busy geocoding this data and working on other various mapping projects using the data.

We noticed one day that one of the shopping center points was off. It was off by like 10 miles! A google search, followed by a visit to the REIT's

---

[1] http://events.esri.com/conference/sagList/?fa=Detail&SID=1551

[2] https://spglobal.com/marketintelligence/en/index

website showed the correct location. I remembered seeing somewhere that S&P Global had a $50 error guarantee (and they still do today).[3] We sent the error in with a map pointing to the correct location from the incorrect location. Next thing we knew we get an e-mail back that reads, "yes your error has been accepted and your $50 gift card is on the way." There were over 13,000 records at the time. Over the next 10 months or so we spent nights and weekends working through the database. And it was not just shopping centers, there were apartments, storage unit developments, even ski resorts! By using a nationwide aerial photo layer from Esri's[4] ArcGIS Online we were able to zoom in on each location and see from the aerial if the point was in the correct location. As a result, I can look at any aerial today and automatically spot all of the apartments, shopping centers, and storage unit developments. We systematically worked through that database and I believe that today (partly as a result of our work) S&P Global has one the best geographic databases on the market. And interestingly enough, most GIS analysts in the real estate industry business (even analysts from companies that subscribe to S&P Global) still don't even know about it.

After surviving the Great Recession that started in late 2008, I decided to leave in 2012 to start a location analytics consulting group with a fellow GIS coworker at the time named George Daigh. Today our group is called Beitz and Daigh Geographics. A year later Todd Atkins, also from EDENS, came and joined our group as a partner. Both of my previous employer's company names were based on the founder's names, so we went with the name even though it bucked the current trend of short mostly meaningless names.

Running a location analytics firm has been challenging and interesting. Early on we became an Esri Business Partner, and they have been great to work with. It's been fun to see what clients want to do and then to get to help them do it. One of the first big projects we worked on involved Esri and some site selection/location analytics work for a new Whole Foods location. Ahead of the International Council of Shopping Centers (ICSC) RECon conference in the summer of 2013, Esri asked us

---

[3] https://spglobal.com/marketintelligence/en/campaigns/quality-program

[4] http://esri.com/

to create a location analytics and marketing package for Whole Foods to come to Redlands, California. In between other projects we spent months on this project. At the end we sent it to a Whole Foods broker, the director of research at Whole Foods, the Economic Development Director at the city of Redlands and we sent it to a successful Whole Foods developer in Atlanta. We almost instantly started getting feedback on the project. At ICSCS Recon in Las Vegas, Nevada the real estate developer met with us and the cities' economic development director. After the conference the developer went to meet with the President of Esri, Mr. Jack Dangermond, to discuss some ways to work together on this project. Several years passed with little info on the project moving forward. Then we spoke with Mr. Dangermond at the Esri user conference in 2016. He mentioned that they were currently looking at two grocery retailers for the site. About a year later it was announced that the retailer Sprouts was going to be the grocery anchor. After the store opened, Mr. Dangermond let us know that it was one of the best openings saleswise that the retailer had ever had.

Acknowledgments

Special thanks to my wife and business partners, George Daigh and Todd Atkins, for their continued support of this book. I also would like to thank all our Planned Grocery® advisors and clients for their continued support of the data and platform.

Introduction

A lot has been written on Business Intelligence and Information Technology. Using data analysis in the decision-making process is common for most medium to large organizations. Organizations are also doing a better job of eliminating silos of data and streamlining the capture and sharing of data throughout the organization. I personally love to see it when organizations become more efficient just by organizing their data and improving their workflows. Conversely it drives me crazy every time I go to the doctor and they ask me to fill out the same information over and over. They even duplicate the data they are asking for over multiple pages! Now the last time I was there they had iPads with a couple of fields already filled in. Now that's making progress, but something tells me we still aren't quite there in the health care sector. The real estate industry has historically been a laggard in information technology. This is surprising since when you think about it, real estate is an industry that operates on information inefficiencies. If you have even purchased or leased real estate, then you know what I mean. Think of all the data you must gather to complete a real estate transaction. Who has the advantage here? Someone that works in real estate everyday like an agent or landlord, or a small business owner leasing a space for the first time?

I recently watched an Apple event online where they introduced all the new products. This usually happens in the fall and they live stream these events to get as much press attention as possible. There was something very interesting that I noticed at the beginning of the presentation. They showed the location of the building where the event was taking place and mentioned the name of the venue and city that it's located in. Now Apple is very meticulous about these presentations and I wondered why they did this. I think they did this because they designed the presentation to have the core elements of a story. People remember stories better than facts. Stories take place in settings; and settings depend on location. I think the location of the building being in San Francisco also helped to reinforce the Apple brand. When you think of adjectives to describe Apple and San

Francisco, many of the same words come up: Cool, Beautiful, Expensive, and Diverse. Location brings context to your story. Think of a picture of the Grand Canyon with a dusty winding trail in the middle of the summer. Now think of a picture of Times Square, New York in the winter at dusk. Each place has a group of unique data characteristics based on its location. Now this is all great for a book or a movie, what does this have to do with business data?

Business organizations are trying to solve problems every day to become more successful. Often when these problems involve data sets that contain the aspect of location; groups either skip or get bogged down into how to include location in the analysis. Obstacles can include lack of data and software, or simply the lack of knowledge of the options for integrating location analytics into your organization's enterprise workflow. This book is designed to prepare you to recognize and take advantage of situations where you and your organization can become more successful through the use of location analytics.

Geographic Information Systems (GIS) are the foundation for location analytics. GIS consists of layers of spatial data that are overlaid to perform analysis and/or data visualization. Dr. Roger Tomlinson (1933–2014) is generally recognized as the "father of GIS." He developed the first GIS for use by the Canada Land Inventory in the early 1960s during which time he was working as a photo interpreter for Spartan Air Services in Canada. When tasked with identifying the best location for a tree plantation in Kenya, Tomlinson worked with computers to find a solution. He went on to sell this solution to the Canada Land Inventory who assisted the government with land use and land planning. His GIS methods greatly improved the accuracy and efficiency of working on land use projects at the time.

Location analytics is simply the analysis of location data displayed in order to communicate a specific measured result. This analysis can be done on a small scale such as—"What are the demographics of my stores that have the best sales?" Or it can be done on a large scale such as—"Which parcels in a specific state have the best soils and necessary slope for a new large-scale farming project?" Increasingly these projects and platforms are moving from a single analyst or group of power users to enterprise systems that are used by many people in the organization. As these enterprise systems grow so does the complexity of integrating these projects. Having good data to work with makes a huge difference in accuracy of the project, as well as in the time it takes to deliver a completed project.

Paul Amos, previously the Managing Director of the Wharton GIS Research Laboratory at the University of Pennsylvania and with over 18 years of experience with GIS and real estate, defines location analytics as "the study of variables that are pertinent to the success or failure of a real estate location." And Mr. Amos goes onto say

> On an individual level, people use location analytics for where they choose to live. In addition to their preference for the type of dwelling (e.g., Condo, single-family, rent vs. own, etc.), they may consider factors near where they are locating such as access to parks or cultural attractions, school district quality, crime and taxes. Commercial businesses use location analytics to identify concentrations of customers that would most likely purchase their products. They may also be interested in knowing the location of complimentary and competitor locations, traffic patterns and site characteristics. Industrial firms may use location analytics to identify areas with qualified employees based on the company's human resource needs along with logistics options to move their goods from the industrial facility to the locations where the products are sold. Firms that can take advantage of new and unique databases can gain a competitive advantage with location analytics. I've seen growing availability of international demographic databases which can certainly help a multi-national company with their location analytics needs. The precision of these databases is not as detailed to small geographic regions like census block groups in the US or postal codes in Canada. I'm sure these databases will continue to be enhanced and much like a real imagery was 10 years ago, these data will become more commonplace and inexpensive as the adoption rate increases.

The Shopping Center Group, headquartered in Atlanta, GA, has been using location analytics for a while now to find the best locations for various retailers. Working with retailers and landlords alike, The Shopping

Center Group is in the business of making the most of location data. As Director of Innovation and Technology at The Shopping Center Group, Gregg Katz says that

> I can tell you that what we have learned is that to truly work with, and understand, location analytics you need to understand the movement of the consumer: what is the true trade area of a location, where are people traveling from to get to a location (home/work/other), what times of day does a location get the most visits. Does a retailer want to cannibalize because the net result is better than the current situation? We have concluded that location analytics is a combination of demographics, psychographics (consumer behavior) and understanding movement. Combine this with local market knowledge and you have a winning formula.

Gregg goes on to say

> Understanding holes in the market, cannibalization, trends, and so on. As with Landlords, I will again reiterate that all of this information cannot be looked at in a silo. It must be combined with a local market understanding based on "boots on the ground" research. Information is only useful if you use the right information and accurate information. Just because a computer says "it is" does not mean it has taken everything into consideration. Examples include roadwork, retail shifts because of new developments, and so on. That is most often not reflected in location analytics from a data perspective. Location analytics does a good job of showing you what is but does not factor in what's next without adding a formulaic/algorithmic approach to it and even that can be hit or miss and take years and a lot of money to perfect.

Whatever the size or scale of the project, there are several elements that are key to perform this analysis. GIS software is at the heart of performing and displaying location analytics projects. GIS requires spatial analysis software, location data, and computer hardware to run and share the analysis. The results of this analysis include various outputs such as a map, table, report, interactive web-map, and/or an interactive web-based dashboard that includes any combination of these elements. There are many options when it comes to GIS software and data; the key is pick the software and data that best fits your organization's goals for the project as well the budget limitations. Keep in mind that sometimes a "point in time" solution might solve an immediate need but does not provide an ongoing long-term solution.

Market and Markets, a leading market research and consulting firm, has determined that the location analytics market is estimated to grow from $6.83 billion in 2014 to $11.84 billion in 2019, at a Compound Annual Growth Rate (CAGR) of 11.6 percent from 2014 to 2019.[1] And they go onto say that

> In terms of regions, North America is expected to be the biggest market in terms of revenue contribution, while emerging econo-mies such as Middle East and Africa (MEA), Latin America (LA), and Asia-Pacific (APAC) are expected to experience increased market traction with high CAGRs, in the due course.

---

[1] http://marketsandmarkets.com/PressReleases/location-analytics.asp

CHAPTER 1

How to Recognize Spatial Problems and Opportunities by Becoming a "Spatial Thinker"

Now that you have an overview of location analytics it's time to train your thinking to recognize when this methodology can be properly used. Location analytics stands for the analysis, measure, and display of location data. This term can apply to many different business categories other than just real estate. So how do you learn to recognize when to take advantage of this powerful tool? One way is to review case studies and articles on how others have used location analytics to solve problems or improve business operations. Later in this book we will go into some of these more detailed case studies. Another way is to train your brain to recognize spatial data sources as well as have an understanding of the analysis you can perform when you combine these geospatial data layers. You will be amazed at how much free data is out there, and you will be frustrated by the inconsistency of data availability from similar organizations. For example, one county will have a lot of free data available and then the county adjacent to it will charge so much for that data that it becomes unaffordable for your project. There is a lot of controversy over this. Since the government created the data in the first place many argue that they can't charge for something that the taxpayer has already paid for. Others point out that the data should be available under the "Freedom of Information Act." In any case, you will have to be prepared for this inconsistency if you deal with data produced by a county government organization.

Figure 1.1 below shows how information on the earth's surface is organized into data layers. Those data layers can then be interacted with in a GIS mapping program.

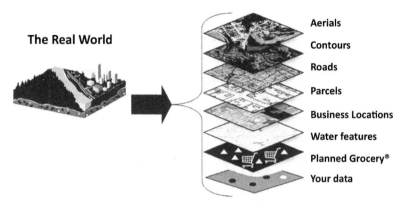

Figure 1.1 Example of how the real world translates to GIS layers

Spatial thinking requires you to look at problems as layers of data stacked together. For example, if you need the population of a one-mile radius from location. First you need the location—this is a point layer, then you need a radius—this is a circle polygon layer, now you need a demographics layer—this is another polygon layer. If you stack the radius layer over the demographics layer—then you can use GIS to aggregate the proportional population to the radius. Think of the radius as a cookie-cutter; the radius will carve out the proportional population from the demographics layer and assign it to the radius layer.

Now think about a shopping center for example. How many layers of data can you imagine would surround a shopping center? Shopping centers have parcel boundaries that carry zoning restrictions. They also have value based on rents and cap rates. Shopping centers have demographics, traffic counts, parking spaces, and light poles. Each retailer in the center has a customer trade area composed of the customer's home and work locations. All the retailers in the center also have different lease financial terms, separate lease restrictions, and varying lease durations with varying options for renewals. Much of this data is spatial or at least tied to spatial data features. Spatial thinking requires you to not only consider the physical spatial data features but also the associated data attributes as well because many enterprise systems have links to non-spatial data that are in linked tables.

Imagine that you work for a shopping center real estate company. What spatial problems might you be asked to solve and what opportunities might there be to use location analytics? First, that depends on the level of sophistication of the company's GIS, its integration with other company data systems, and the level of detail and accuracy of their data. Creating a demographics table from the shopping center point locations would be fairly simple but totaling the parking spaces of the shopping center portfolio or finding the total square footage of asphalt in the property portfolio would require a very detailed property data set. Creating a trade area for each center would be difficult without having any data on where the center's customers are coming from and knowing how much they spend. With the right retailer data sets, like the data from AggData LLC[1] for example, an analyst could perform a gap analysis to see what retailers are missing from any given market. This analysis would then be used by the leasing department to gauge the interest of retailers to fill space in the shopping center.

Mr. Paul Amos, who at the time of writing this book was Director of the Wharton GIS Research Laboratory at the University of Pennsylvania, spoke to me about business opportunities for spatial thinkers working at companies that are expanding internationally: "Firms that can take advantage of new and unique databases can gain a competitive advantage with location analytics. I've seen growing availability of international demographic databases which can certainly help a multi-national company with their location analytics needs. The precision of these databases are not as detailed to small geographic regions like census block groups in the US or postal codes in Canada. I'm sure these databases will continue to be enhanced and much like a real imagery was 10 years ago, these data will become more commonplace and inexpensive as the adoption rate increases," said Mr. Amos.

Here at Beitz and Daigh Geographics we have a product called the "Opportunity Surface™" that is used mostly for real estate market analysis. Opportunity surface puts spatial thinking to use by combining all the necessary locational elements into layers that are then overlaid onto a grid for scoring. From this we can produce a map or aerial that highlights the areas that best meet the combination of those elements. For example, many real estate analysts evaluate locations based on the demographics of

---

[1] https://aggdata.com/

a three-mile radius. But to find the locations with the best demographics it is not practical to run three-mile demographics one by one for thousands of locations. This is where the grid (Opportunity Surface™) comes in. For a city we create a grid with quarter mile (0.25) grid boxes. Each grid is 0.25 square miles. One city can have thousands of grids. Then we use the GIS to create centroids of each grid. A centroid is the center point of each grid. This centroid layer is then used to run three-mile demographics for each point. Then we calculate demographics for each three-mile radius. Most often for real estate we look at population, income, education, and number of employees (otherwise known as daytime population). Then we score the radius based on weights of the demographic variables. The results are then appended back to the grid so we can create color coded (thematic) maps that highlight grids with the best scores.

Below in Figure 1.2 we have a grid analysis that we did for a company that was looking for locations with demographics similar to Chipotle Mexican Grill and Panera Bread for the Indianapolis metropolitan statistical area. First, we ran eight-minute drive times for the Chipotle Mexican Grills and Panera Breads in the area. We chose eight minutes because we felt that was a fairly accurate standard trade area. From there we looked at the median incomes, total populations, and daytime populations

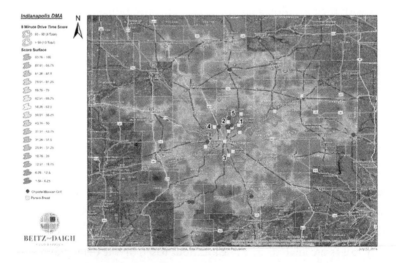

Figure 1.2 Opportunity Surface™ example showing top 5 best locations based on criteria

(employment) for these stores and came up with scoring based on those variables. The scoring weighted the variables so that the areas with similar population, daytime population, and incomes would score well. Then we ran a 0.25-mile grid for the area, calculated the centroids of the grids, and ran eight-minute drive times from all of the grid centroids. Lastly, we scored the eight-minute drive time trade areas to see which trade areas scored the best. The numbers 1, 2, 3, and 4 in Figure 1.2 indicate the four highest scoring trade areas.

A good spatial thinker combines industry and data knowledge with a solid understanding of the capabilities of GIS software analysis. They strive to create and maintain accurate data sets and never miss an opportunity to capture data points if that data will be valuable or will save time down the road. Many organizations have unrecognized spatial data sets that are the key to unlocking future growth. Spatial thinkers learn to seek out these data sets and then mine them for ways to create value for the organization.

CHAPTER 2

Location Analytics Project Development

First it helps to understand the steps involved in assessing and then implementing a location analytics project. In the next chapter, I'll tell you about a retail real estate marketing project that my consulting group Beitz and Daigh Geographics, Inc. worked on and you will see these steps first hand. But first let's look at the basic steps in a location analytics project.

Here is a basic outline of the steps in the process:

1. Start with your questions and goals
2. Determine your study area
3. Assess your data requirements
4. Assess your software and 3rd party services need
5. Check the budget to see if it all works
6. Create a phased approach if necessary
7. Perform the analysis and recalibrate as necessary
8. Evaluate results
9. Create a plan to communicate and act on your findings

Project Start

Once you have recognized an opportunity to use location analytics then it's time to get your project going. If you work for a large organization be careful to not let the scope get too big for your project. Often companies get stuck at the beginning of a project by creating an unusually large scope of work. If the scope gets very large, then break the project into phases so you can get the project going. Taking it slow by implementing a solid phase 1 will go a long way toward your success. I have seen many companies try and do too many things at one time, and they end up doing nothing partially well. Then you have a bunch of half-done phases trying to connect and it turns into a disaster. You may also consider creating a request for proposal (RPF) that details your requirements. This way you can shop the RPF to several companies to better compare pricing, timing, and approaches. If you are doing this project internally then it still helps to have a scope of work or project goals document. This way you can clearly communicate the goals of the project, stay on task, and highlight areas where the project needs improvement.

Study Area

Determine your study area early. There is nothing worse than creating a great project only to have your client come back and ask "But what about this state or that city?" Set clear expectations early on what and where the project will cover. Sometimes your study area will be determined by the data available. You may want to slightly broaden your study area depending on the project. For example, a South Carolina project could include Charlotte, NC and Augusta, GA because those cities have a direct effect on cities in South Carolina that are close by.

Data

Next you need to evaluate the data required for your project. If you need data for your project, then you need to determine where it's coming from and how much it will cost. Do this first by evaluating what data sources and data subscriptions you have in-house. Are there other departments in the organization that have data you can use or data that they can create for the project?

Government entities are great sources of data since they often have the budgets, staff, and the need to create and maintain large diverse spatial data sets. Most cities and counties have data sets that deal with infrastructure and property. Many states maintain data sets on aerial imagery, contours, soils, and wetlands. If this data is free, then it is usually available for download at the organization's website. If the organization charges for data, then there are usually instructions on cost and who to contact to get the data. Florida, North Carolina, and California are three states where data is often readily available and free at the state and county levels. If you have a relatively small study area, then going county by county for parcel data might be feasible. Or if you only need the locations of grocery stores within a small city then you could build this data set as well easily by collecting all the names and addresses of the stores and geocoding them into the GIS.

But what if you need parcels for several states? Or if you need the entire portfolios of a retailer's locations? Private companies have many great data sets available to help with these needs. If you need retailer locations, then AggData, Chain XY, Trade Dimensions, and Chain Store Guide are great companies to consider. With over 6,000 layers in 35 countries, AggData has one of the largest retailer databases on the market today. With a premium subscription to AggData, this data is also accessible via Esri ArcGIS Online. What this means is that if you are working in Esri ArcGIS Desktop or Esri ArcGIS Online then you can directly import these retailer layers without the need to geocode the raw files. If you are looking for parcel data then Real Estate Portal USA, Digital Map Products, and Corelogic are worth checking out. Maponics is a data provider company that has some great neighborhood, social place, and school attendance zone boundary GIS layers. Companies like Trulia, Redfin, eHarmony, and Angie's List use data sets like these to better help their customers engage with their services.

Demographics data is another data set that many companies use for location analytics projects. Much of this basic data is free from the census, but it can be difficult to assemble into a GIS program and it lags the current year estimates and projects provided by other companies.

In a move to strengthen its presence in the business sector, Esri purchased the demographic company CACI in 2002 and used it to create a business information systems solutions division called Esri BIS (which has since been folded into Esri). Today Esri provides demographic data in its Business Analyst Desktop and its Business Analyst Online products. Users can access this demographic data at the various census geographies by viewing it in a color coded (thematic) map or by calculating it for trade areas such as a radius or drive time. STI: PopStats, provided by Synergos Technologies, Inc., is another demographic provider and they are very popular with the real estate site selection community. With quarterly updates, STI: PopStats helps businesses to see where the growth is taking off, compared to other companies that provide only annual updates. Other demographic data providers include Applied Geographic Solutions (AGS) and Nielson.

Demographic data is collected and referenced at the various census geographic entities. A basic understanding of these entities will help in planning a location analytics project. Census Blocks are the smallest level of geography that data is collected at. At this level you get data on population, households, and housing units. The next level up is Census Block Groups. It's at this level where you find the most detail with the most demographic variables. If you are working on a project and you need to aggregate data on a radius or drive-time, then you really need to be working with Census Block Group data.

The Federal Deposit Insurance Corporation (FDIC) has great data sets for banks. This data set not only has all the major bank locations, but it also has data on the annual branch office deposits. Banks themselves can use this data to explore markets for new branches. They can also explore if a specific branch's deposits are increasing or decreasing abnormally compared to the peer banks in the market. Shopping center companies and real estate developers can also use this data to help lure new banks to new or existing developments. A market where the banks have strong deposits or where bank deposits have dramatically increased recently will be a prime market for new bank locations.

The National Center for Education Statistics also has great location data available for public and private schools. These data sets can easily be geocoded, and it includes the number of students and teachers per school. School data is great because it helps show the nodes of activity in a market for families. Retailers take note of this data when working on market planning for new stores. Homebuyers also should take note of this data if they are looking to avoid a street that is frequently traveled in the morning and afternoon by buses and parents transporting students.

ArcGIS Online by Esri has many layers that you can use either as backgrounds or analysis layers. This service also allows users to create new data sets by "geo-enriching" their existing data. For example, if you need to highlight all the stores in an area with high income, but you don't have the latest demographic data then you can "geo-enrich" your data by adding demographics. There is a minimal cost for this through the ArcGIS Online credits payment system, but the cost here is usually not a big concern unless you deal with very large data sets. In the case of large data sets there are other solutions available such as Esri Business Analyst for the desktop. This is an expensive program, but users can run as many demographic requests as the want without having to pay credits on ArcGIS Online.

Tapestry Segmentation[1] data by Esri is another data source to keep in mind for your projects. This data is available down to the block group level and classifies residential neighborhoods into 67 unique segments based on socioeconomic and demographic characteristics. These 67 segments are rolled up into 14 LifeModes in order to summarize the data at a high level. Organizations will find it easier to adopt the 14 LifeModes for the simple reason that they are easier to remember if you are dealing with the general population. If you are only targeting the top two or three LifeModes then it helps to understand the segments that make up those LifeModes. Here is an example of the LifeMode "Uptown Individuals":

LifeMode: Uptown Individuals

- Young, successful singles in the city
- Intelligent (best educated market), hard-working (highest rate of labor force participation) and averse to traditional commitments of marriage and home ownership
- Urban denizens, partial to city life, high-rise apartments and uptown neighborhoods
- Prefer debit cards to credit cards, while paying down student loans
- Green and generous to environmental, cultural, and political organizations
- Internet dependent, from social connections to shopping for groceries (although partial to show rooming)
- Adventurous and open to new experiences and places
- And then within the LifeMode "Uptown Individuals" you find the segment "Laptops and Lattes."

---

[1] http://esri.com/landing-pages/tapestry

Segment: Laptops and Lattes (within LifeMode Uptown Individuals)

General

- Households: 1,240,000
- Average household size: 1.85
- Median age: 36.9
- Median household income: $93,000

Who Are We?

Laptops and Lattes residents are predominantly single, well-educated professionals in business, finance, legal, computer, and entertainment occupations. They are affluent and partial to city living—and its amenities. Neighborhoods are densely populated, primarily located in the cities of large metropolitan areas. Many residents walk, bike, or use public transportation to get to work; a number of work from home. Although single householders technically outnumber couples, this market includes a higher proportion of partner households, including the highest proportion of same-sex couples. Residents are more interested in the stock market than the housing market. Laptops and Lattes residents are cosmopolitan and connected—technologically savvy consumers. They are active and health conscious, and care about the environment.

You can find the full profile with maps and graphs here: http://downloads.esri.com/esri_content_doc/dbl/us/tapestry/segment10.pdf

If you are marketing a product or service to well educated, 30-somethings, living in the city, and who are technically savvy, then this is your group. You would have to study all the profiles in each LifeMode to determine which ones fit your target audience. Or better yet if you have existing data on where your best customers are located then you can use GIS to determine the most represented LifeModes and Segments for your customers who spend the most money. This analysis will show you the top segments for your existing best customers. You can then focus your marketing dollars in those areas that contain your target LifeModes and Segments. Another way to work with Tapestry data is to aggregate the LifeModes and/or Segments by retail spending totals. This is particularly helpful to those in shopping center and retail businesses. For example, if you have a lifestyle center site and you want to show a retailer who the customers are in the surrounding area. You take the site and create a 10-mile radius, then you aggregate or take a summary table for the LifeModes in that radius by retail spending. What you then get is a table that details what LifeModes are the highest spenders in the 10-mile trade area. Of course, this does not account for tourists or anyone living outside the 10-mile radius for that matter, but it does give you a snapshot of the retail spending by LifeMode segment. Figure 2.1 is an example of grocery spending by LifeMode percentage. You can see here that the High Society LifeMode accounts for 30.42 percent of the grocery (or food at home) spending in the 8 minute drive time trade area.

Directory of Major Malls is another data source to keep in mind if you are working in the shopping center sector. This data set contains the locations and information on all significant shopping places in America. Depending on your project needs you could use this data in a variety of ways. Since each location has the square footage you can use the GIS to visualize markets and see where the larger centers are located. Users can also use this data to compare the demographics of a potential shopping center site to the other centers in the market.

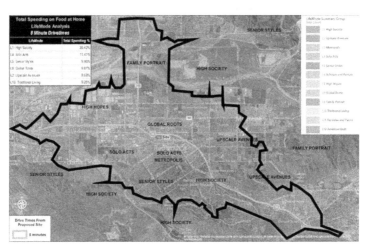

Figure 2.1 Total spending on food at home by LifeMode percentage

Data Sources (Links Current at Time of Publication)

FDIC: https://www2.fdic.gov/idasp/warp_download_all.asp

National Center for Education Statistics—Public Schools: http://nces.ed.gov/ccd/schoolsearch/

National Center for Education Statistics—Private Schools: http://nces.ed.gov/surveys/pss/privateschoolsearch/

Esri Tapestry: http://doc.arcgis.com/en/esri-demographics/data/tapestry-segmentation.htm#ESRI_SECTION1_87F5D845F8E04723AE1F4F502FF3B636

AggData: www.aggdata.com

Chain XY: chainxy.com

Chain Store Guide: https://chainstoreguide.com/

Directory of Major Malls: http://shoppingcenters.com/

Medicare Physician List: https://data.medicare.gov/Physician-Compare/National-Downloadable-File/s63f-csi6

Evaluate Your Software and 3rd Party Services Need

There are many GIS software packages out there for consideration and you need to choose carefully based on your project and data needs. I include data here again because many GIS software packages have various data packages included as well. I'm not going to go into all the packages, but I will give details on the package that I currently use when working with clients.

Here at Beitz and Daigh Geographics we use software and data (including demographic data) from Esri. As an Esri business partner, our location analytics solutions revolve around Esri technology. The desktop software package called Esri Business Analyst is an extremely powerful program. Business Analyst Desktop comes with demographic data and a large selection of tools to perform and display spatial analysis. Business Analyst Desktop also integrates with the web-based Esri ArcGIS Online. ArcGIS Online extends the desktop by providing literally thousands of base maps and data sources for use in the desktop GIS. ArcGIS Online also provides a web-based platform to share your GIS projects. Once you publish a project to ArcGIS Online then you can share that interactive map with other users who can access it via a computer, tablet, or other mobile device. ArcGIS Online also provides a good selection of analysis tools and "geo-enrichment" features. Geo-enrichment provides users the opportunities to add attributes to features. Attributes include items such as the slope of a property or the demographics of a radius. In addition to best in class demographics for the United States and Canada, Esri recently added a significant amount of international countries bringing the total amount of countries available to 137 at the time of the printing of this book.

Depending on the size of your project and the size of your organization you may want to outsource your entire project instead of investing in the software, data, and personnel. This decision is purely based on how often your organization will have to perform this analysis and if you want to develop this expertise in-house. If your core business is not GIS or location analytics focused or if you don't have the funds to sustain a GIS department then you may want to select a location analytics partner to work with. Coming from the Esri world, I would recommend finding a good Esri Business Partner. Our group Beitz and Daigh Geographics would be happy to evaluate your project and if it doesn't fit our profile then we would be happy to recommend another group for your organization to work with.

Getting Started

If you are over budget on your project, then consider a phased approach. Projects of this nature tend to get big at the beginning and often get stuck in "analysis paralysis." The best way to move forward is to phase in the project into steps. Step one needs to be something that gets you going and provides some results that everyone can see. Then for phase 2 you have more information, and often this new information brings up new questions to ask. Phase 2 can be tweaked to incorporate your phase 1 findings, and then the project gets smarter as it moves forward.

After your project is complete, then you need to communicate your results and determine an action plan based on your findings. Often with location analytics projects your results will be map based or web-map based. By creating a web-map of the data created in your findings the stakeholders in the project have a way to explore the findings interactively. It's also a good idea at this point to find a resulting actionable item from the study that can be used to benefit the business. By acting on your findings you can validate the purpose of the project. Then you can also incorporate the results of taking action into your next phase 2.

CHAPTER 3

Integration with Other Business Systems (Business Intelligence Versus Location Analytics)

I would say that location analytics is a niche market in the overall broader business intelligence field. Gartner, a leading IT consulting firm, defines business intelligence as "an umbrella term that includes the applications, infrastructure and tools, and best practices that enable access to and analysis of information to improve and optimize decisions and performance."[1] Location analytics fits well under the business intelligence umbrella because it serves the same purpose, but it requires a specialized set of data and tools to accomplish the goal of improving decisions based on data analysis and data visualization.

Up until now we have mostly been focused on single project location analysis. But what if your organization already has enterprise systems in place that is dealing with large amounts of data? Location analytics can be viewed as an extension of these current systems, an extension that enhances the current data spatially, giving the user added insight into the data. As an Esri business partner, I am most familiar with solutions that are connected to the Esri ecosystem so those are the ones that I will focus on in this book. If you are taking on a large enterprise location analytics project, then I encourage you to explore all the options that are available on the market.

Business intelligence solutions are centered on dashboards, visualizations, and reports that enhance business decisions and help to make the

---

[1] http://gartner.com/it-glossary/business-intelligence-bi/

organization more efficient. IBM Cognos and MicroStrategy are two such systems that integrate with Esri to produce the location analytics elements of business intelligence. These elements include map and aerial content as well as location data content such as demographics, business locations data, heat maps, consumer spending, and lifestyle data. Visualizing the organization's data on a map helps users to see patterns that graphs and charts can't reveal.

Customer relationship management (CRM) data has traditionally been table driven, but Esri's integration with sales force allows users to pull out more insight. Users can understand the demographics of these customers and they can explore the other customers that are nearby a specific place so that time in the field can be spent more effectively. Users can also create heat maps, point clusters, and other data visualizations.

Esri software also integrates with Microsoft Office and Sharepoint. Microsoft Excel spreadsheets with location data can easily be transformed into map views that are embedded into the spreadsheet. Microsoft PowerPoint can be used in the same way to show live interactive maps inside of PowerPoint, so that the presenter does not have leave the application and open a different map browser. Microsoft Office and Share-Point both require an organization subscription to Esri ArcGIS Online for this to work.

CHAPTER 4

Mobile Devices

Mobile devices are having a huge impact on data gathering for location analytics projects. Think of all of those "check-ins" on social media, photos taken that embed location data, and Wi-Fi routers that can collect data from your phone on where you go inside of a retail store. To determine your location, smart phones use a combination of GSP, Bluetooth, Wi-Fi, and cell towers. To check to see if your photo has location coordinates, all you have to do is to look at the properties of the photo in windows for example under "Properties" and you will see the Latitude and Longitude under GPS. On a Mac you can do the same thing by selecting "Get info" and looking under more details.

The real estate industry has benefited greatly from the evolution and sophistication of mobile devices. Paul Amos, previously with the Wharton School Geospatial Initiative, states that:

> Mobile devices are becoming more commonplace in the evaluation of real estate and business applications. Mobile devices can be used to collect information about locations which can be sent to the company for further analysis such as collecting customer intercept surveys as they shop at a store to determine why they traveled to shop at the particular store. Mobile devices are also a great medium for serving content to enable the real estate decision makers in the field to access information that a company feels is most pertinent for its real estate decision process. Accessing information from a company's servers through a mobile device improves the speed and efficiency of the real estate professional by having access to information anytime and anywhere.

One great mobile app for real estate is Esri's Business Analyst Online. This app allows users to evaluate sites, trade areas, and/or neighborhoods

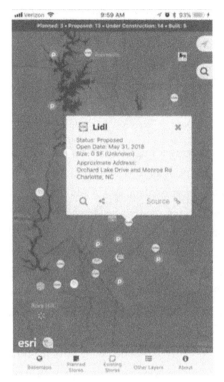

Figure 4.1 Planned Grocery® mobile application

for 135+ countries. Users can tap into a large collection of demographic data sets, reports, and maps. This app also allows for collection of data in the field that can then be retrieved when back in the office. Another mobile app for real estate is the app we built for the Planned Grocery® application. Figure 4.1 shows a screen shot of the Planned Grocery® mobile application. Users can have the app display their location while moving and then the app shows them the nearby locations of grocery stores that are proposed, planned, under construction, and recently built.

CHAPTER 5

Business Location Analytics Applications for Various Industries

It's estimated and commonly accepted that about 80 percent of an organization's data has some type of spatial component. Today, industries are evolving their information technology and business intelligence operations by adding location analytics. This evolution is taking form in the use of map- and aerial-based enterprise dashboards, as well as in the form of specific project-based location analysis. From here we will look at some various industries and how they are using location analytics. Organizations with well-organized data and who are already strong in the business intelligence area are best poised to add location analytics to their workflows and decision-making process.

Agriculture

As of the 2007 census of agriculture, there were 2.2 million farms in the United States covering an area of 922 million acres. Agriculture is big business, and it's not just the large staples like corn, wheat, and soybeans that most of us think of. It's vineyards, pine trees, and increasingly marijuana in some states. In addition to farms, the Census Bureau estimated in 2003 that 94.6 percent of the United States is rural open space. This is a huge market when it comes to determining the highest and best use of this real estate and for optimizing the existing farmland to find the maximum productivity and probability. Location analytics can be used here in several interesting ways.

1. Agricultural Planning: Geographic information system (GIS) layers of data are combined to support decisions on what to plant and

how to harvest. For example, an agriculture company could use GIS to find land suitable for planning vineyards that are capable of being machine harvested. The land would have a specific slope threshold (so the machines can still operate) as well as the variables of soils composition, and sun exposure. A leading seed provider has taken this a step further by creating an online seed recommendation platform. Clients of this seed company can input variables into a location analytics platform (that the seed provider hosts) so that the correct crops are recommended based on the land conditions and any other local data that the farmer has.

2. Agricultural Management: Deciding when and how to harvest a crop, how to irrigate, and how to apply pesticides all fall under management. Here location-based data can be used to visualize the current land needs. A timber company for example can take a parcel of land and look at the site index data, combined with knowing the year the stand was planted, for a given tree type such as loblolly pine and get an idea on when that tree stand needs to be harvested. This information brings cost savings when planning the management for many tracts of land across several states for example.

Financial Services

Banks must be accessible to their customer's needs. While technology is making the traditional bank branch less frequently used, the bank branch still serves a significant purpose for interacting with customers to provide financial services. Here are some ways that location analytics can be used in the financial services industry:

1. Bank branch planning and reallocation: Banks can monitor their customers and evaluate locations in a similar way that retailers do. Each bank branch has a customer list composed of addresses and the corresponding financial products associated with that household. Banks can map out the trade area for each branch to see which areas have the most customers using a particular bank branch. Doing this type of mapping can also help pinpoint the neighborhoods that have the most profitable customers. After these neighborhoods are

identified then the bank can determine if they should alter their marketing plans specifically to target these neighborhoods or see if there are enough of a new customer base to open a new location altogether.

2. Target Marketing: Banks can also use location research to study the demographics of customers who are using certain financial services and then use targeted marketing to market to market to customers with similar demographics. For example, a bank can take a customer list of people who are using a certain financial service and map their locations in a GIS demographics program. The mapping program can then be used to come up with a demographic profile of who is using that service. Once the demographic profile is created, then the same mapping program can be used to highlight other areas in the city that match those target demographics. Then those highlighted areas can be targeted with mailers, phone calls, or other marketing.

Economic Development

Luring the right company to a location is a big deal. There are many vocations throughout local and state government, as well as private industry, whose jobs are dedicated to this purpose. Today, data drives decision making more than ever and the decision to locate somewhere involves a good bit of location-based data. Here are some ways that location analytics can be used with economic development.

1. Real estate web-mapping platforms: Many government entities provide web-mapping platforms to show locations that are intended for development. These locations might be government supported mega sites intended for industrial use or large business parts, or they might be privately owned real estate where the owner is seeking the highest and best use of the real estate. In any case, location analytics can be used to show a variety of attributes for each site such as demographics, traffic counts, drive time distances, wetlands, floodplains, and access to rail and interstates. The South Carolina Department of Commerce (https://locatesc.com/) for example, has a great web-mapping application that shows the availability of land

and industrial buildings. Each location has a map, sales price, and size of the building or property to start with. Then the user can click for a pdf that has the full property details such as zoning, flood zone status, elevation, soils, utilities status, and transportation statistics such as nearest port, airport, intermodal facility, rail access, barge access, and runway access.

2. Location Marketing: In the same way governments encourage economic development, private real estate developers also have an incentive to bring business to the state. These developers often use marketing packages to show why a site is the right fit for a particular use. For example, a developer might create a package for a new grocery anchored shopping center. This package would show a map overview, a neighborhood overview including any existing and planned grocery competition, a site aerial with traffic counts, a demographics report, and maybe some thematic (color-coded) heat maps showing the population growth, population density, and average household income. These packages are either created in-house or they are tasked out to marketing and research firms like our business here at Beitz and Daigh Geographics.

Hospital and Health Systems

A well-known early example of spatial data analysis involved an English physician named John Snow. In 1854, he mapped out those in London who were affected by cholera. The results of the maps then led him to discover the location of the well that was causing the disease. Location analytics in Hospital and Health Systems can help health workers to better understand how environmental factors affect the health of individuals. Data on health provider locations can also help health workers to identify neighborhoods that need better access to health care.

1. Public Health: Hospital systems can work with government agencies to identify populations that need health services. This can be done by studying emergency room visit rates compared to the distribution of health care facilities and looking at the demographics of the neighborhoods. Maybe a neighborhood has a disproportionate

population of elderly people or the people in the neighborhood do not have good access to public transportation. Understanding the "where?" helps us to ask the right "why?" questions.

2. Geomedicine: Location factors can often influence a person's health. Geomedicine is used to help bridge the gap in information used by medical personnel to diagnose heal issues. It's estimated that the average American moves over 10 times in a lifetime. That's at least 10 places, or 20 if you count a separate work location, where the environment can influence a person's health. When medical personnel have this information, they are better equipped to diagnose illnesses.

Insurance

To adequately plan for risk, Insurance companies must better understand the events that can cause disruption. Earthquakes, flood, and severe weather are just several elements with predisposed location sensitivity. But location analytics can also be used in insurance by looking at driving habits via GPS data, and the use of aerial imagery to evaluate insurance claims. Here are some ways that insurance companies are using location data to better understand risk and to serve customers better.

1. Risk Assessment: If you live near an active fault line then your property is more likely to experience damage in the event of an earthquake. If you are on the coast in a low area near a river that feeds into the ocean, then you are more likely to experience property damage from flooding during a hurricane storm surge. Lastly if you live in "tornado alley" then you best be prepared for higher insurance rates compared to people who live outside of a severe weather area. All of these are examples of locations of areas that are predisposed to location sensitivity.

2. Driving Data Analysis: The Progressive Insurance Company offers a program for customers called "Snapshot." Optional enrolment in this program requires enrollees to install a GPS data collection device into the automobiles diagnostic port. Since car insurance rates are based on historical information on people such as age and car type, Snapshot digs deeper into how people actually drive. From the

Progressive website under the Snapshot details for South Carolina, here is how the data is used:

"How Snapshot affects your insurance rate

Your Snapshot driving results are reviewed at two points: after collecting 30 days of data and at the end of your driving period. Safer driving habits can help you earn a discount of one percent to 30 percent. Riskier driving habits will not lead to a discount, but there is no change to your premium. While your driving results are set at the end of your driving period, your corresponding discount percentage may change over time."

Progressive goes on to detail what data is collected and how it is used: "What we use to calculate your Snapshot result

Hard braking—Hard brakes are decreases in speed of seven mph per second or greater. Your Snapshot device will 'beep' when you brake hard. Minimize hard braking to work toward a discount.

Mileage—Total distance of trips. To earn a discount, try to minimize your time behind the wheel by combining trips, carpooling or using public transportation.

Time and day—The number of minutes you spend driving during higher risk hours—the highest risk are between midnight and 4 a.m."

I have not seen any data released on how many people get discounts after having the device evaluate their driving data, but after reading some online comments it seems that the device helps Progressive to find the people that really don't drive very much at all and it's those people that get the best discounts.

3. Crop Insurance Fraud: The U.S. Department of Agriculture (USDA) helps farms to manage risk through the Federal Crop Insurance Program (FCIC). In cases where the FCIC suspects that fraud is involved, they can use location analytics data to review the claim. Landsat satellite imagery is used to determine if the farmer planted the field in the first place then the imagery can also be used to estimate the area of damage to the field.

Location-Based Services

Location-based services are data driven services based on the user's location. For example, when you ask Siri for the nearest restaurant or you download the GasBuddy app to look for the best price on gas nearby. Both services return results based on the user's current location. Foursquare was an early adopter of collecting user's location data and they made a game out of checking in to various places. I was the "Mayor" on Foursquare at my old workplace for a while until someone else checked in more times than me and they stole it from me!

1. GassBuddy: The GassBuddy app is a great example of crowd sourced data redistributed to users based on their location. This app works in real time, so users can always find the best gas prices nearby. The app displays locations of gas stations nearby with the latest gas prices. It's estimated that GassBuddy has 70 million users.

2. Apple's Siri: In addition to Siri showing the nearest restaurants or whatever else you are looking for, people can also use Siri's location feature to set location-based reminders. For example, you can get Siri to remind you to pick up milk when you drive by the grocery store or remind you to call someone as soon as you arrive at work. All you have to do is to name these locations with specific names in your contacts with addresses.

3. Roadside Assistance: Many roadside assistance companies provide an app that tracks the user's location so service can be provided faster without having to get directions from the user.

4. Uber: Uber reinvented travel by combining mobile access, mobile payments, and location-based services. The Uber app tells drivers your pickup and dropoff locations. When your ride is complete the user is charged the fare on their credit card.

Logistics

Companies that must deal with route planning and fleet management use location analytics to improve operations. The Internet of things (IoT) also allows for introducing sensors such as temperature and weight to factor into the equation. This powerful combination allows for improved efficiency across the supply-chain.

1. Shipping: Route management is an important part of the shipping process. So is making sure that the trucks are property loaded and not overweight. Route management is a location analytics process in that it uses software that can maximize efficiency by providing the drivers the most direct route for getting from one point to the next. Live weather data layered into this software also helps drivers to be re-routed during weather events that may delay a shipment. But shipping involves much more than route management. Fleet management enables companies to match the right driver to the right truck for the job. Imagine if a shipment needs to be kept a temperature, or if the driver needs a certain skill set such as driving on the ice tundra in Alaska, or if the driver needs a government clearance to make a delivery. These variables can be tracked and matched correctly so long as the data is kept up to date. Now imagine that a driver is on route to deliver some pharmaceuticals to a government facility that are required to be cooled and the shipment is time sensitive. A large storm is predicted for the northern route of the trip, so the driver takes the southern route. Then a sensor shows that the temperature is rising on the shipment, a closer look shows a faulty fuse is to blame and the truck is routed to the nearest repair facility. After getting the fuse fixed the driver is able finish the route and enter the government facility because he has the proper clearance.

Marketing

Getting your message to the right people at the right time is very challenging. The Internet has changed forever how and where people consume media and how they communicate. But at the same time, more and more data is available to work with and there are more targeted platforms than ever to reach consumers and or other businesses.

1. Direct mail: Direct mail is still a powerful marketing tool when done right. Location analytics software can be used to match the

message to the right customers. One good example of software that does this well is Esri's Business Analyst Desktop software. Let's say that your company just built a very high-end shopping center and you want to help drive traffic and awareness of the new location. To maximize your marketing dollars, you decide to send a shopping bag to 1,000 people instead of mailer to 10,000 people. Those 1,000 people will be targeted using GIS software to isolate the shopping bag shipments only to people who live in the highest income neighborhoods. Another example follows the logic that people generally like to shop at the same places as their neighbors. Let's say that you open a specialized burger place and you have a point of sale system or app that collects your customer's location data and amount spent on each transaction. After several months of being open you decide to analyze this data using location analytics software. You geocode the customers and build the trade area based on who spends the most at your restaurant. You then use that trade area to send out mailers with a coupon for coming to check out your restaurant.

Media and Entertainment

If a picture is worth a thousand words, then a map can be worth a million words. Maps take the results of location analytics research and boil those results into images that are easily understood.

1. Journalism: Journalists can use maps to show how data is changing the landscape of places. For example, a map with shading that shows which counties in a state have the highest unemployment. Or more complex examples like the maps produced by FlowingData using data from AggData. They did a great exhibit a while back showing the distribution of grocery store chains across the United States— here is that example: https://flowingdata.com/2013/06/26/grocery-store-geography/. By incorporating location data into stories, journalists can enrich their stories and make them easier for readers to understand.

Mining and Petroleum

The Mining and Petroleum industry benefits greatly from combining information that they collect and create with data that is publicly available from the government and other data providers. Location analytics platforms enable these companies to gather this data and share it throughout the organization as well as out into the field.

1. Exploration: By mapping drilling sample data, users can see patterns that help them to chart where to explore next.
2. Pipeline Maintenance: With thousands of miles of pipeline often running through remote areas it can be a challenge to keep up the maintenance of these lines. These companies are using location analytics applications to monitor these lines. A plane will fly the route of the pipeline and a person will use a mobile device to mark on the aerial any places that need to be checked out on foot. This data is then sent real time to people on the ground so that they can plan trips to visit these areas in person. Mapping applications can also be used to analyze change in aerial imagery around these pipelines.

Ports and Maritime

Ports are the lifeline of the United States economy. Having the ability to import and export goods helps drive commerce and all our major retailers depend on these goods coming in to fill their store inventories.

1. Operations Overview: Dashboards like CommandBridge by Ares Security (formerly Mariner) for example, enable port operations staff to have a broad view of all that is going on at a particular port. These dashboards combine GPS data on ships coming and going, along with cameras stationed throughout the port. Data on buildings within the port can also be loaded into the system.

Real Estate

Real Estate is an area that is very well suited for location analytics applications and analysis. Real estate construction alone contributed $990 billion to the *nation's economic output in 2015.*[1] *Real estate especially is an industry that operates on information inefficiencies so the more data that can be captured and shared throughout the organization the more effective that organization will be.*

1. Market studies: Colliers International is a real estate services company with some of the best market studies in the industry. You can find their searchable database here: http://colliers.com/en-us/insights/research-the-market. These studies are broken out into categories such as health care, hospitality, industrial, land, multifamily, office, residential, retail, and specialty. Location analytics data collected and displayed in these reports includes information on the square footage vacancy, inventory, and absorption in the market. Low vacancy rates and rising rental rates are a signal that new construction may be coming soon.

2. Site Selection: Companies can use location analytics software in lots of ways to support site selection depending on the level of sophistication of the company and what type of industry they are in. Home builders focus on employment drivers (jobs and where they are located) as well as school districts. Retailers especially focus on population, income, and traffic counts. Location analytics platforms can be used by organizations to collect and distribute location data and location analytics research results. Opportunity Surface™ by Beitz and Daigh Geographics (mentioned earlier in this book) is one example. For this solution a market is broken down to grid cells and then drive times are generated for the centroid of each cell. The demographics are then calculated for each drive time and each drive time is scored based on the scoring criteria. These scores are then linked back to the grid cells and the results are displayed color coded (also known as thematically).

3. Information Technology driven Marketing Automation: There is a huge opportunity here for companies to save time and have better results in their marketing efforts. Shopping Center Companies have

---

[1] http://useconomy.about.com/od/grossdomesticproduct/f/Real_estate_faq.htm

been struggling with data overload for some time. Many of these companies have hundreds of properties and those properties have thousands of tenants. Since the tenants are changing all the time, so are the site plans, the website, the leases, and internal data that is kept by various departments such as property management, leasing, development, marketing, and construction. The opportunity here is for companies to store this data in one place and then use location analytics applications to display that updated information on the site plans themselves. So whenever a site plan is opened it will always have the latest information. Beitz and Daigh Geographics has done some work in this area and has a solution called OneSite Pro™. Property Capsule is another company doing great work in this area.

Real Estate Data and Information Platforms

There are lots of data providers with real estate data. It can be hard to figure out which ones to use and how to navigate pricing and user licenses. There is also a lot of talk out there about new platforms that are disrupting the real estate industry. In fact, there are entire conferences dedicated to this. Disrupt CRE and CRE Tech conferences are both held annually throughout the year in many major cities. Below are some companies and solutions worth noting (and one of them is provided from Beitz and Daigh Geographics so I am a little biased).

1. Planned Grocery: Chapter 8 describes this application in depth, but in a nutshell this subscription platform and iOS app tracks the planned grocery store locations across the United States on an interactive map. The existing grocery store locations are also included so that users can see areas that are missing existing and planned stores. This helps with site selection and it also helps organizations (especially grocery chains) to plan for competitive openings that might affect the sales of nearby store locations.

2. AggData: Over 6,000 lists of business location data. Top companies across the United States use this data for site selection and have it included in various platforms. Chris Hathaway is the president and he's been at this for a while. For example—if you want a list of all the

Whole Foods locations, they have this list with latitudes and longitudes so that it can be imported into mapping programs. At the time of the writing of this book the Whole Foods list is just $99. Compare that price to the time it would take to scrape the Whole Foods website and geocode that list. Aggdata also has Premium subscription which allows organizations to pull as much data as want for a set fee each year. Premium subscribers who are Esri users also get access to the data through Esri's ArcGIS Online, making the data even more accessible and easier to use.

3. Esri Business Analyst Online (BAO): A great platform for running demographic reports. A subscription to Esri's ArcGIS Online is required first. The mobile app for BAO is also great for running demos on the go. Users of BAO can analyze trade areas, do color-coded thematic mapping, and perform map searches that reveal areas that match multiple demographic variables.

4. REPortal USA: Affordable parcel data available for purchase one county at a time if need be. REPortal also has a great app called LandGlide that runs $10 a month. From this app you can zoom into any location that has parcel coverage and you can look up the ownership and see an aerial of that parcel. Digital Map Products and CoreLogic also have great parcel data.

5. CartoFront: This is a subscription platform dedicated to site selection and property information with coverage mostly in the Chicago area at this time. Unlike your basic county map property look up, CartoFront layers in many information sources including legislative actions that may affect property values. Originally named Herbfront with a focus on the legal cannabis real estate market, Cartofront is a good example of a location analytics business that has pivoted to appeal to a broader market.

6. Directory of Major Malls: Over 8,300 major shopping centers and malls with the ability to search by store name, ownership, geography, and demographics. Directory of Major Malls also contains 315,000 associated store locations, 4,200 site/leasing plans and 23,000+ primary retail real estate contacts.[2] Having used a stripped down version

---

[2] https://shoppingcenters.com/who-we-are

of this data in Esri's Business Analyst Desktop software, I can say that this is great data to use if you are in the retail real estate industry.

7. CoStar/LoopNet: A monster of real estate data. They have a lot of great office and retail leasing data for purchase via a subscription. CoStar has the best data I have ever seen dealing with retail square footage. If you want to see for example the total retail square footage for a certain city or neighborhood, then CoStar has the best data for this. Subscribers can see for example when a certain lease is set to expire. This gives a leasing agent an advantage in that they can contact the tenant and see if the tenant wants to move to a new location and get better lease terms. CoStar purchased LoopNet a while back. LoopNet is the biggest online platform for finding commercial properties to lease or buy. Commercial real estate brokers often list their properties on LoopNet.

8. HanleyWood/MetroStudy: The best source for location based residential subdivision data on the market. Subdivision data is broken down into number of units planned, number of units built, and price point ranges. They cover most major markets across the United States.

9. REIS: Detailed reports including vacancy rates, rent levels, cap rates, new construction, rent comparables, sales comparables, valuation estimates, and capital market trends across eight real estate categories including: Flex/R&D, Self-Storage, Apartment, Office, Seniors Housing, Retail, Student Housing, and Warehouse/Distribution.

10. SNL: Now a part of S&P Global and the data company I mentioned in the preface, SNL focuses its data and reports into the following five categories: Financial Institutions, Real Estate, Energy, Media/Communications, and Metals & Mining. The Real Estate data is very detailed, and it includes an export feature with latitudes and longitudes in the records so that the data can be mapped and analyzed in location analytics software applications. Users can also use the mapping built into the SNL platform which won a Special Achievement Award in GIS from Esri in 2012.

11. Census Bureau: Free location-based government data available at census.gov. TIGER is just one data source here and has a rich history

of being the first nationwide digital map available for use in GIS. From the census website:

TIGER is celebrating its 25th anniversary. The Topologically Integrated Geographic Encoding and Referencing database—the first nationwide digital map of roads, boundaries, and other features—was initially created for the 1990 Census to modernize the once-a-decade head count. However, its impact went well beyond its initial purpose by offering common map data in electronic form that powers the GIS industry today. Through its TIGER/Line products, the Census Bureau has provided the common geospatial framework for use in linking statistical and other data in GIS.

The idea for TIGER developed within the Census Bureau. In the 1970s mathematicians, geographers, and software developers designed a spatial data handling system that resembled one big spreadsheet. Custom-built solutions were the norm for most GIS software companies in the two decades leading up to TIGER's release. TIGER was like a giant interlocking puzzle on which hundreds of people worked, bringing together different pieces to create a single, seamless map. Besides its national scope, what set TIGER apart was topology—a unique way of assuring accurate linkage of spatial relationships between geographic entities—and TIGER did this on a grand, national scale, bringing structure and order to the pre-TIGER world of "digital chaos." But, TIGER could not rest. Staying relevant within the fast-moving geospatial data world that it helped create, TIGER had to continue to improve and evolve. In TIGER's second decade, the Census Bureau linked TIGER with its Master Address File. The spatial accuracy of TIGER was greatly enhanced to make use of GPS in Census operations and to facilitate digital exchange of data.

The end result of this huge collaborative effort for the 1990 Census was a database that contained a latitude/longitude-coordinate for more than 30 million feature intersections and end points and nearly 145 million feature "shape" points that defined the more than 42 million feature segments that outlined more than 12 million polygons. It was a monumental task that succeeded. TIGER was the first "big data" solution to manage every level of U.S. geography down to the block level for all states and territories (Puerto Rico and Island Areas). Its maximum size then was measured in gigabytes. Currently the TIGER database is 25 terabytes.[3]

Retail

Retail is the largest private employer in the United States. Retail directly and indirectly supports 42 million jobs, provides $1.6 trillion in labor income and contributes $2.6 trillion annually to U.S. GDP.[4] Retailers can use location analytics to improve and support various operations. These operations are similar to functions mentioned earlier in the real estate section, but there are some functions that are unique to retail only.

1. Indoor Mapping: Retailers can create hot spots of where their customers spend most of the time in their stores. Mobile devices register anonymous location data points that can be analyzed and mapped. This is done by working with the wifi router data. When retailers see the results of this analysis, they then can change the merchandise layout accordingly. By developing multiple hot spots in a store, customers will then be drawn by other products that they might not normally see, thus increasing the potential for additional sales.

2. Merchandise Selection: Depending on the retailer, some stores have the option to customize merchandise at each location to some degree. By understanding the demographics that are unique to each location, stores can vary the merchandise to appeal to nearby customers. For example, if the incomes and net worth are high nearby then in general that store will support higher quality and higher priced items. Also understanding the colors of nearby sports teams has helped some stores to connect better with customers. By increasing the color selection of inventory to reflect the colors of nearby high

---

[3] http://census.maps.arcgis.com/apps/MapJournal/index.html?appid=2b9a7b69 23a940db84172d6de138eb7e

[4] https://nrf.com/resources/retail-library/the-economic-impact-of-the-us-retail-industry

school and college teams, retailers can better connect with the community and provide products that nearby customers are looking for.

3. Marketing: Point of sale systems and loyalty programs are collecting more data today on customers than ever before. Customer spotting allows retailers to see this distribution of customers on a map. Retailers can use this data to better understand where the best customers live and then direct market to those neighborhoods.

4. Focus Groups: Retailers and shopping center developers can use location data to their advantage when conducting focus group sessions. This is done by understanding what tapestry segmentation groups your focus group subjects come from and making sure that you have an even distribution of the people you want to ask questions of. By mapping out and assigning tapestry segmentation to your available pool of focus group attendees you avoid getting responses from people that are similar or all grouped together living near the same place.

Telecommunications

Mobile phones, cable service, Internet, and (least we forget) landlines, are services that we all depend on every day. Location analytics helps companies to increase the quality of telecommunications services and to improve customer service.

1. Service Routing: Cable companies can use location analytics to improve customer service visits. By routing service visits based on driving time and estimated time to complete each task, companies can provide shorter windows for customers to sit around and wait for service.

2. Cell Towers: Mobile phone providers can map out population density with existing tower locations to find spots where new towers need to be located. In addition, they can overlay customers phone data to see where "dead zones" are. Imagine a map color-coded by LTE vs. 3G signal reception. This data visualization helps companies to make better decisions.

CHAPTER 6

Top 5 Retailers Based on SuperZips Study

In early 2014, our consulting group Beitz and Daigh Geographics teamed up with data provider AggData to study retail locations were most prevalent in the United States Super Zips. Author and social historian Charles Murray first coined the term Super Zips in his analysis of the nation's zip codes in relation to their percentile ranks in college education and in income. The zip code's ranking is a number between 0 and 99 representing the average of its percentile ranks in college education and in income. Using 2013 income and population data from Esri, the 1,097 zip codes with rankings of 95 and higher are identified as Super Zips.

By taking AggData's database of nationwide restaurants and overlaying them using Geographic Information System (GIS) on the Super Zips, this gives an interesting look into which restaurant chains have the highest penetration into this elite demographic. This study focuses on 294 restaurant chains with 50 or more locations in the United States and looks at the chains that have the highest percent of inclusion in the Super Zips.

Here are the results of the study:

1. Pret A Manger—75 percent of Pret's locations fall within a Super Zip. Pret started in London in 1986 and its first location in America opened near the New York Stock Exchange in 2000. This restaurant concept is known as a "cross between a good restaurant, an Italian coffee bar and a bullet train."

2. Cozi—59.34 percent of Cozi's locations within a Super Zip. Cosi started in 1996 with one restaurant based on a small Parisian Café. Today Cosi is a place with a "comfortable, urbane and contemporary atmosphere ... A place where all elements combine to stimulate the senses and create a lasting impression."

3. Jerry's Subs & Pizza—46.77 percent of Jerry's Subs & Pizza's locations fall within a Super Zip. Jerry's Subs & Pizza's is an American fast casual sandwich and pizza restaurant chain based in the Washington, DC metropolitan area. First store opened in 1954 outside of Washington, DC. Self-described as "more than a sandwich shop. It is more than a pizza shop. It is America's two hottest franchise concepts rolled into one. In addition to our signature line of specialty cheese steaks, our menu features a variety of overstuffed subs, pizza, and related food items that are both delicious and unique."

4. Zpizza—45.24 percent of Zpizza's locations fall within a Super Zip. Founded in Laguna Beach, California and in business over 25 years, Zpizza falls into the category of "better-for-you pizza ... the largest gourmet pizza franchise in the world that features fresh, organic ingredients."

5. Corner Bakery Café—40.37 percent of Corner Bakery Cafe's locations fall within a Super Zip. Opened 1991 in Chicago, IL. This restaurant is a place "with real kitchens in place of assembly lines; over 40 types of fresh herbs, fruits and vegetables; a real panini grill; and ovens that work all day long to deliver freshly baked breads and desserts."

Keep in mind that this analysis is done at the zip code level. Zip codes can have large disparities in income and education levels based on specific locations within the zip code. This Super Zips analysis of income and education could be performed at the block group level of geography to increase accuracy. Also, for a different way to view the data, this analysis can even be performed with drive times and custom trade areas around portfolios of stores and/or shopping centers. By using this analysis, real estate professionals can learn more about their own properties or the properties of retailers that they are targeting for potential deals.

CHAPTER 7

Predictive Location Analytics: The PetSmart Acquisition of Petco

In the fall of 2015 news broke that PetSmart was looking to acquire Petco. Our consulting group Beitz and Daigh Geographic's thought it would be interesting to look at these store portfolios and study the location analytics of this merger. According to the latest data from AggData, at that time, there were 1,440 PetSmart locations and 1,292 Petco locations (including 127 stores under the Unleashed by Petco brand).

Since this was just a study more geared to marketing our capabilities, we decided to only focus on the stores in the continental United States. Using Esri Business Analyst Desktop GIS software we discovered that 62 percent of Petco locations are within a 10-minute drive time of a PetSmart. Drilling down even further we found that there were 223 Petco locations (17 percent) within 1 mile of an existing PetSmart, and two PetSmart locations contain two Petcos each within a one-mile radius. We next focused our analysis on these 223 "overlap" locations at the 10-minute drive time trade area and noted some interesting findings by looking at the Market Potential Data from Esri.

The Market Potential data showed that PetSmart had a much higher household market share than Petco does, when it came to households who "purchased pet supplies." Looking at the overlap stores, only four of PetSmart's trade areas report more customers buying pet supplies at Petco than PetSmart (two of these stores are in Los Angeles and two are in Chicago), while the majority (219 stores) report more customers buying pet supplies at PetSmart than Petco. Revenue numbers seem to validate this data in that roughly over the past 12 months; PetSmart's revenue #'s was close to $7 billion in the 12 months to February 1, 2015 and Petco's

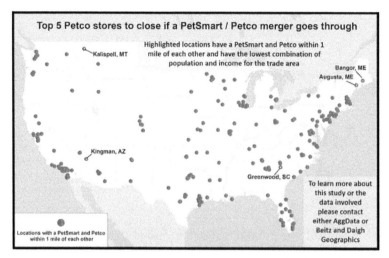

Figure 7.1 PetSmart and Petco merger location analytics analysis

were close to $4 Billion in sales in the 12 months to January 3, 2015.[1] The Market Potential data is provided in Esri Business Analyst desktop and the information originates from consumer surveys complied by GfK MRI.

When retail chains merge, store closures often result. Next, we looked at the population and income for all the 10-minute trade areas for the overlap stores and highlighted the stores that have the lowest combination of population and income. This map in Figure 7.1 shows the top five locations where a Petco would most likely close (assuming the merger goes through and that the weaker market share store would close):

Petco's stores tend to be smaller and more neighborhood oriented, while PetSmart's stores tend to be larger and located in big box centers. Also, Petco sells a broader range of animals compared to PetSmart, and Petco is perceived as more expensive in general compared to PetSmart. Time will only tell if the merger goes through and these targeted stores identified in the analysis are closed.

---

[1] http://reuters.com/article/2015/09/18/us-petco-m-a-petsmart-idUSKCN-0RI23A20150918

CHAPTER 8

Planned Grocery® (A Real Estate Location Analytics Platform)

Grocery retail is changing faster today than ever. Technology, delivery, meal kits, and in-store special amenities are just some of the things that are changing consumer behaviors. Behaviors that traditional real estate companies have depended on for years. This evolution will impact store sizes, layouts, merchandise mix, and most importantly store locations. Planned Grocery® is the only platform on the market today that specifically tracks planned grocery store locations nationwide. Already in use by some of the best-known grocery retailers, shopping center owners, real estate developers, and investment banks across the country, this platform makes it easy to see new store expansion and contraction trends in the industry. This combination of data gives subscribers a never before seen look at the current nationwide grocery expansion. Figure 8.1 shows the Planned Grocery® platform starting view of when the application is first opened. Each logo represents a grocery store that is either proposed, planned, under construction, or recently built in the last six months.

Beitz and Daigh Geographics (of whom I am a partner in the business) started creating the data for the Planned Grocery® platform in early 2014. Working with various retail real estate clients throughout the United States, we kept running across the locations of planned grocery stores that had yet to start construction. I knew that real estate companies were doing this research only for the trade areas that they were interested in. I also had never seen a nationwide layer just for these sites where grocery stores were planned for. So, I started a GIS layer for these and then kept adding locations as I found them. Originally this layer was an ESRI shape file where I worked with it in the Esri ArcGIS Desktop software. After some time, we uploaded this layer to Esri ArcGIS online where more editors

Figure 8.1 Planned Grocery® location analytics platform

could work with the data at the same time and from outside of the office. We then had some interns at that time and they started researching and adding these locations as well. Any time I had some extra time that was not directly related to another project I would start adding to and refining the data in this layer. We classified new locations as planned, proposed, under construction, and recently built (within the past six months). And later we added a dead deals classification for sites where a grocery store was planned but then the deal did not move forward.

News articles are our primary source of finding these locations. We developed a search algorithm to help find these planned grocery locations and we developed an audit methodology to keep the data up to date. We also source data from social media, planning organizations, the grocery retailers themselves, as well as real estate developers. If the source mentions that the site is speculative or that the site still needs to clear hurdles such as a zooming change or approval from city or county council, then we mark that location as proposed. We mark the location as planned if the source document says the location is planned and will likely start construction soon. If the ground is being prepared or if building is going up, then we mark the location as under construction. When the location is built and open for business then we mark the location as built. We also capture the square footage, the source on the web, the accuracy of

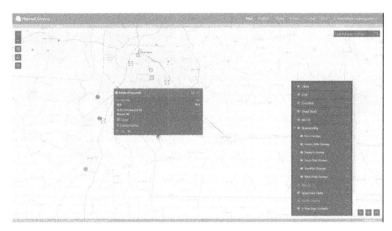

Figure 8.2 Planned Grocery® platform showing a proposed Publix info box

the location, the square footage, the developer, source url for marketing materials, and the attributes of the location itself. Figure 8.2 shows a view of the Planned Grocery® platform with a proposed Publix info box.

Later that year in 2014 when we had hundreds of locations, Todd Atkins, a partner in the business and our developer at Beitz and Daigh Geographics, built the web-mapping platform to incorporate this data. He also later created an iOS version of the app for the Apple Store. At this point we needed a logo, website, and some brochures, so one of our interns recommended a designer he knew who recently graduated from the University of South Carolina. This guy did amazing work on helping us get everything going and looking great. The first retail developer that I showed the platform to in my office in January 2016 subscribed right on the spot. Special thanks go out to Frank Cason with Cason Development for becoming Planned Grocery® customer #1! Shortly after this we added a major grocery chain (who prefers to remain anonymous) and then we added Ledbetter Properties who are shopping center owners and developers. In May of 2016, I remember going to the Gravisite Site Selection conference (formally the Gravitec Site Selection conference) in Clearwater, FL where Jim Puffer graciously offered for us to show the platform in one of the breakout sessions. I got up early that morning to add more locations to the database. It was that morning that we crossed over 1,000 locations. Shortly after this we went on to add the clients

Wegmans, MTN Retail Advisors, RAM Real Estate, Lowes Foods, and Whole Foods. Our goal was to get 10 users in 12 months and we hit 10 users in half that time. Later that year we went on to several more conferences and continued to consistently add clients.

Pricing has been a difficult part of the equation to figure out. We originally thought the platform should run about $10,000 a year. But after several conversations with developers we decided to market it at $2,500 a year for the login version, with an extra annual cost for additional users. We went on to create two other pricing levels as well. We have a streaming data plan where we stream the data into our client's mapping applications and they have the option to login to our platform as well. If they are an existing Esri client, then this is very easy and can be set up in no time. If they use a different mapping technology, then we can provide them API access to the data. Presently our streaming plan partners that include Esri, TETRAD, SiteZues, eSite, and Intalytics. We also have a raw data plan that includes logins to the platform, streaming, and the ability to download the raw data from the application. We recently raised prices at all pricing levels to help pay for the continuing maintenance of the data the costs associated with adding new layers to the platform, as well as costs associated with application (Web and iOS) development.

With solid market validation we did an official launch in the fall of 2016. For 2017 we kept adding new subscribers and almost tripled our income that year compared to 2016. The year 2017 was great, we were mentioned in the *Wall Street Journal* and *Business Insider* and we started worked on the next version of the platform. The next version of the platform just recently launched (at the time of writing this book) on March 12, 2018. It took us over five months to finish this major update. Todd did most of the work. We added a nationwide parcel layer that displays the lot lines and shows parcel ID, ownership data, and the parcel's acreage. Figure 8.3 shows the Planned Grocery® platform with the new parcel layer on the aerial base map. We also added a layer of data from Space Jam Data which shows who wants what grocery retail and where. Space Jam Data performs social media surveys across the United States for various property owners and developers. After meeting with them in New York at the International Council of Shopping Centers (ICSC) NY Deal Making conference we formed a partnership include their data in our platform in

Figure 8.3 Planned Grocery® platform showing aerial view with parcel data

exchange for adding some links to their website for our clients to follow in case they want more information on their services. We also added e-mail alerts so that our clients can opt in to receive a daily e-mail showing them new locations that we have recently added to the platform. Lastly, we added a "Newsworthy" section that includes locations that are slated to close. Presently this includes all Toys R Us locations and 94 locations owned by Southeastern Grocery which includes the Bi-Lo, Win Dixie, Fresco y Mas, and Harveys Supermarkets.

The Planned Grocery® platform was originally built with WordPress and Esri's ArcGIS Online. Then for version 2.0 we dropped Wordpress and replaced it with our own code (when I say we I mean Todd). This platform contains the existing grocery store locations as well. For the existing grocery store locations, we scrape retailer's websites to get the most up to date data as possible. We added three options for base maps: Light, Dark, and Bing Hybrid Aerials. The platform has four thematic demographic layers: Five Year Population Growth, Population Density, Average Household Income, and Esri's Tapestry Segmentation. We also include traffic counts, county boundaries, and core based statistical areas from the census. When you have one of the demographic layers turned on and click one of the sections you will see a pop-up window that tells you the dominant tapestry segment with a link to the full tapestry description. This pop-up also shows the percentage of people that have completed a

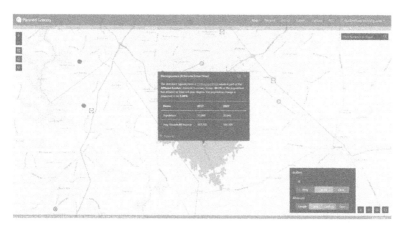

*Figure 8.4 Planned Grocery® platform showing a drive time analysis
with demographics*

bachelor's degree and higher, along with stats for income, population,
and population density. The platform has measurement tools for area,
distance, and for capturing the latitude and longitude of any place on
the map. Other tools include the ability to calculate basic demographics
for a radius ring and drive time polygon. Figure 8.4 shows the Planned
Grocery® platform with drive time demographics.

In the summer of 2018, Planned Grocery® was accepted into the Esri
Marketplace. The Esri Marketplace is designed to make it easier for users
to find data and applications for use with ArcGIS Online subscriptions.
Currently our "data streaming" plan falls into this usage but being listed in
the Esri Marketplace makes it easier for Esri users to find us and see what
the data is all about. Esri users can also purchase an annual subscription
to the Planned Grocery® data set directly through the Esri Marketplace.

Our platform is subscriber driven in that we take feedback from our
users and update the platform based on their suggestions. In May 2018,
we had a booth at ICSC RECon for the second year in a row. This was
our busiest conference so far. Clients and interested parties in the platform continue to give us lots of great feedback on improvements to make
to the data and to the platform itself. We are currently looking at adding
more reporting and map export functions. There are some other layers
we are looking into adding that will help with site selection, and we have
some great new ideas for ways to improve the Planned Grocery® iOS
mobile app.

CHAPTER 9

Solar Farm Site Selection with National Land Realty

Today there are over half a million solar installations operating in the United States and experts agree that this industry is ripe for continued growth and innovation. But what happens when a high-tech industry collides with the historically low-tech relationship driven real estate industry? Solar providers know the technology and financial part of the equation to continue to change the face of renewable energy, but in many cases, they are slowed down by the real estate process of qualifying sites and negotiating property leases.

Solar companies ran into such a problem several years ago when they set out to grow their solar facility networks on the East Coast. For a site to qualify for a solar facility, more than a dozen separate location-based criteria must be analyzed and scored. The property owner for a potential site would also have to be contacted to see if they were interested in leasing or selling the land. The problem was that many properties were available for lease or sale but did not qualify for solar. Then for the sites that did fully qualify for solar only a small percentage of owners were interested in leasing or selling their property. These solar companies and the rural real estate brokerage business discovered that they had a location analytics problem and National Land Realty set out to solve it.

In early 2014, National Land Realty, working with several solar energy companies, started a pilot project with Beitz and Daigh Geographics to find a solution. With North Carolina as a testing ground, the solution was developed over several months and entailed using a combination of GIS and data driven processes that rank parcel sites based into the categories of *Prequalified*, *Qualified*, and *Not Qualified* status. Dean Sinatra, COO of National Land Realty at the time, lead the charge to create a data driven process for efficiently finding qualified sites, contacting the owners, and tracking the data for each potential deal. With millions of land parcels across the United States he knew that a single county or state solution would not work. They needed a highly scalable multi-user analysis and data collection platform; combined with a process for shifting through all the location data. Early on they could tell that a solar companies' detailed property analysis would not be needed unless they had an interested land owner, but they did not want to work with the land owners until they thought the land might be suitable for a solar farm development, thus the genesis of a "Prequalified" site. Figure 9.1 shows National Land Realty's Solar Site Selection Platform which is used to prequalify sites for solar farm developments.

To prequalify sites, analysts examine parcels on a county by county basis. The parcels were then prequalified on two basic criteria: Is the site within an acceptable distance of the required electric facility infrastructure? And are there environmental issues that would impede development? If positive results were found for these criteria, then the site would be marked in the database as prequalified. Then letters would be sent out to owners of prequalified sites. If the owner responds and is interested in leasing or selling, then the full qualification analysis would proceed with all the results recorded in the database. Beitz and Daigh Geographics, the GIS consultants for National Land Realty, set out to create a platform to

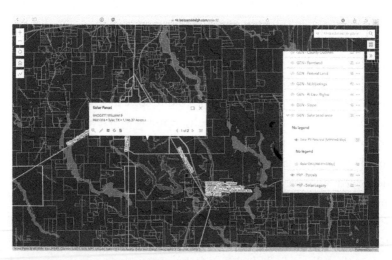

Figure 9.1 National Land Realty's Solar Site Selection Platform

aid in the *Prequalification* and *Qualification* process. The initial solution began with ArcGIS Online and ArcGIS Desktop with layers of data from both Esri and other third-party data sources. The pilot project showed good results with properties being qualified and leases being signed.

As the project looked to scale beyond a single state, Beitz and Daigh migrated the platform from Esri ArcGIS Online to an Esri ArcGIS Server solution hosted originally on the Microsoft Azure cloud and later moved to Amazon Web Services. A customized multi-user mapping application was developed which allowed analysts to prequalify and qualify sites from a web browser or mobile device. Additionally, new functionality was included that allowed analysts to export kmz files which are required for the leasing process, slope and elevation analysis, and parcel searching. Since the application is multi-user with information stored in a central database, "data silos" are minimized and the chances of redundant analysis on a given parcel are eliminated.

Many sites are now prequalified each month resulting in a significant conversion rate to signed leases. Location analytics combined with a real estate workflow is helping to solve this location analytics problem and will help bring solar energy to a grid near you soon.

CHAPTER 10

Eastdil Secured (Real Estate Investment Banking)

Eastdil Secured is one of the oldest real estate investment banks in the industry. My business partner and I started working with them early after we got Beitz and Daigh Geographics started. Considered a pioneer in the industry, Eastdil Secured has participated in every real estate cycle since 1967, attaining over 40 years of real estate investment banking experience. For an example of the impact that they have on the real estate market—over the past 12 months (in 2014) Eastdil Secured has completed over 725 transactions totaling $244 billion. While they include Office, Hospitality, Multifamily, Industrial, Land, and Retail as product types, it is Retail where they have really been using location analytics.

Retail Shopping Centers have an inherent calculated value based on the leases they carry and the value of the buildings and the land. Leases with long terms and national strong credit tenants are very desirable to investors looking to buy shopping centers. So, a shopping center can look great on paper when you look at it today, but what about the center's long-term ability to generate lease renewals and new leases? And how do you communicate a shopping center's location assets that are outside of some pro-forma?

Often when a shopping center is put on the market for sale, an Offering Memorandum book is created that details all the information about the shopping center. The typical items included in these offering memorandums are site plans, rent rolls, and financial statements. For certain shopping centers, Eastdil Secured uses location analytics to take this a step further and explore the location attributes that help drive sales at a shopping centers. Location analytics helps Eastdil Secured to visualize this data through various maps exhibits such as:

- The shopping center's trade area boundaries with statistics on population makeup.
- The locations of the surrounding retail clusters and competition.
- Heat maps showing where the population is increasing or decreasing near the shopping center.
- Aerials showing the clusters of "high spending" households *households with over $100,000 household income per year.
- Anchor tenant demographics compared to the same anchor tenant in nearby markets.

Having the ability to create these visuals provides an extra layer of insight and understanding to would-be shopping center buyers. Location analytics data on shopping centers provides more information to help owners and brokers to craft a data informed story on these properties. This is not only helpful for the short-term sale but also extends onto the leasing and redevelopment process. Materials from the offering memorandum can be morphed into marketing materials that show potential retailers why this property works for them. Retailers love nuggets of good market data because this makes their lives easier when trying to better understand a property.

CHAPTER 11

Dataminr (Real-Time Information Discovery)

Founded in 2009, Dataminr uses location analytics to transform the Twitter stream and other public data sets into actionable signals, discovering must-know information in real-time for clients in Finance, the Public Sector, News, Security and Crisis Management. With over 150 employees (2016), Dataminr is headquartered in New York City, with offices in DC, London, San Francisco, and Montana. Using proprietary algorithms, Dataminr instantly analyzes all public tweets and other publicly available data to deliver the earliest signals for breaking news, real-world events, off the radar context and perspective, and emerging trends.

Dataminr's clustering and event processing engine distills over 500 million tweets a day down to the handful of signals that are valuable to the user. They classify signals based on geo-location, topic relevancy, and market moving implications and rank them by level of urgency.

These real-time signals are delivered via a Web Browser, Instant Messenger, e-mail, Mobile App or can be integrated into an organizations workflow using Dataminr's custom API.

Dataminr for News helps the newsroom keep an eye on all of Twitter, alerting journalists to real-time leads for them to investigate further. Journalists don't have to watch a stream of information—the most actionable Tweets find them, including the ones they don't know they're looking for. Dataminr for News is an enterprise application, with applicability across the newsroom. News professionals can define personalized signals based upon the user's particular topics of interest and regions of focus. Signals are delivered automatically via the application, e-mail, instant message, and integration into internal systems. Dataminr for News was developed in partnership with Twitter. Figure 11.1 is an illustration of how Dataminr's alerts are pushed out through various channels such as

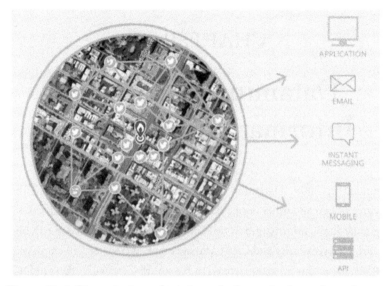

Figure 11.1 Dataminr's analysis is pushed out via alerts through various channels

e-mail, instant messaging, application programming interface (API), and the Dataminr platform.

Financial Services professionals use Dataminr for Finance to act on early market moving information, to gather information from non-traditional sources, and to conduct deeper research from a perspective and timeliness that only Dataminr and our unique data set can provide. Dataminr for Finance delivers a relevant stream of content to financial professionals based upon their personalized portfolio of tickers, sectors, and macro topics. This provides financial users with a new source of alpha, as well as key insights, off-the-radar context, and differentiated perspective.

Transit Disruption News Alert Example

Breaking Alert: Amtrack Train Derailment—within minutes of an Amtrack Northeast Regional train derailing outside of Philadelphia, Dataminr alerted users to tweets sent from passengers still inside the overturned cars. Dataminr detected the earliest signal to the fatal crash 15 minutes ahead of major news reports. Once emergency responders arrived at the scene, Dataminr surfaced valuable updates from the crash site as new and relevant information emerged.

Mergers and Acquisitions News Alert Example

M&A Speculation NOK: Dataminr alerted clients to chatter surrounding Nokia participating in possible advanced negotiations to acquire Alcatel-0Lucents's wireless assets 40 minutes ahead of major news reports. Nokia closed up nearly 3 percent following revelations of a possible acquisition.

Dataminr is an extreme example of the use of location analytics in business. Dataminr's clients directly benefit from the real-time data alerts that are sent according to the client's specifications. Now that the company has just raised $130 million (March 2015) in new funding, be on the lookout for potentially new location analytics services as they move forward.

CHAPTER 12

Placed (Consumer Location Analytics)

Placed is an interesting location analytics company. Headquartered in Seattle, Washington and backed by Madrona Venture Group, Placed provides retailer insights based on data collected from the Placed app called the Panel App. I downloaded the app and it asked me for some personal information. I'm guessing this information is similar to questions asked if I was enrolled in a "secret shopper" program. Placed is evolving the collection of shopping data by providing awards for people who share their shopping patterns and personal information. Placed has several product offerings:

Placed Insights: Placed Insights reports location analytics data through their ratings service which measures the physical world. With an audience of more than one million opted-in users sharing nearly one billion locations a day, Placed Insights provides businesses with the data they need to make informed decisions based on location.[1] Data in this application shows retailers how customers move in the real world and what their preferences are. This data also shows opportunities for cross-promotion. For example, the data might show a group of people who always go to Whole Foods after they work out at a specific gym. A new Sprouts that just opened up nearby could advertise at the gym and try to lure these people into a new shopping pattern. Figure 12.1 shows how Placed Insights ranks retailers based on foot traffic.

Placed Attribution: This product ties online, mobile, and out of home advertising to in-store visits. Placed has over 100 partners including agencies, publishers, networks, demand side platforms, and out-of-home media companies.

---

[1] https://placed.com/products/insights-use-cases

Figure 12.1 *Placed Insights shows the retailers busiest day by month of the year*

Placed Targeting: Mobile target marketing beyond the geo-fence. Geo-fence marketing is where an app sends a targeted marketing message when a mobile device gets within a specific distance of the retail location. Placed targeting specializes in reaching customers while they are still in the decision-making process and not in proximity of the retail stores. An example of this would be to send coupons for a new lunch spot to office workers at around 11:30 a.m. when they are just starting to think about lunch plans.

Placed 100:[2] The Placed 100 is a monthly rank of US businesses based on foot traffic as measured and normalized through the opt-in Panel App, each business report includes details on business rank, category rank, trend, businesses visited, and apps installed.

Placed Affiliate: This program encourages other location-based apps to add the SDK code from the Panel app along with user opt-in language. This allows for greater market coverage beyond the Panel App alone. In exchange for implementing the SDK, the developer of the app earns incremental income.

---

[2] https://placed.com/placed-top-100

CHAPTER 13

Esri (Mapping and Analytics Software)

Headquartered in Redlands, California, Esri is a pioneer in location analytics software and the resulting applications. Today more than 350,000 organizations worldwide rely on Esri software. Jack Dangermond is Esri's CEO; he co-founded the company with his wife Laura in 1969. Part of what makes Esri unique is the ingrained passion they have for making the world a better place. You hear this phrase said a lot, "making the world a better place," but from the messaging at the Esri Annual Conferences to the millions of dollars of free software Esri donates each year to nonprofits/nongovernment organizations (NGOs), Esri not only talks about it, but also they live it as well. As many as 13,000 NGOs from all over the world have used the software to study the Earth's ecosystems to better protect the environment. This includes projects such as monitoring rainforest destruction, cataloging wetlands, and helping to track water pollution back to its sources. David Yarnold, Audubon president and CEO, has said "It's hard to imagine any company that has done more for conservation planning than Esri." STEM education is another area that Esri supports. Esri has pledged $1 billion in STEM software to 100,000 K-12 U.S. schools.

The heart of Esri's software revolves around ArcGIS family of products. These products allow for spatial analysis, app creation, data production and visualization, remote sensing, and 3D animation. ArcGIS Online is the web-component that provides the backbone to share all this data either publicly and/or just within an organization. The Planned Grocery® platform that I mentioned earlier is hosted on Esri's ArcGIS Online. The data for this app is also updated using ArcGIS Online. For location analysis, ArcGIS Desktop and ArcGIS Online can both be used. If an organization needs to created static maps then they often use ArcGIS Desktop, but if they want to publish an interactive map online, then they often organize the data on ArcGIS Desktop and then publish it out to ArcGIS Online.

Esri's Business Analyst desktop software is designed specifically for business tasks. Many of these tasks are wizard driven and the software comes loaded with demographic data, major shopping center locations, Tapestry segmentation data, street base maps, business locations, market potential, retail marketplace, and consumer spending. Specific tasks that the software help perform are: site selection, Geocoding, market planning, territory planning, marketing, thematic (color-coded) mapping, gravity modeling, and market analysis. This software comes with technical support, data and software updates, as well as complimentary Esri User Conference registration. If you are looking for demographic data, then Esri is one of the top companies to consider.

The Esri User Conference is held by Esri annually each summer in San Diego. This week-long conference is where Esri makes its latest announcements. They also have many class sessions on how to use the software in different ways and there are many paper presentations on how people are working with the software. This conference is very well done and well attended with around 15,000 people attending from all over the world each year. Aside from the opening day and various classes there is map display social, lightning talks, and a big party on last night.

CHAPTER 14

Gravitech Development (Gravity Modeling)

Another great location analytics company is Gravitec Development. Their products are specifically focused on site selection for the grocery and convenience store industry. James Puffer founded the company in 1993 when he purchased all the software copyrights from Howard L. Green & Associates. With Mr. Puffer's experience at Retail Systems, Inc. in Minneapolis, he was able to create the first Windows-based gravity modeling system for supermarkets. The SITESPLUS product is still used today by most supermarket companies in the United States.

Grocery stores spend a lot of time trying to correctly project the sales of a new store and trying to project the sales of existing stores whenever a competitor opens nearby. Users of SITESPLUS upload specialized demographic data at the block group level. This specialized demographics data is created by combining normal demographic data (usually provided from Synergos Technologies) with modeling data provided from DSR Marketing Systems. When combined, this data consists of estimates of the dollars spent per person per week. Today in the United States this number averages around $50. Next the competition is loaded into the software and the competition's estimated sales are entered. This often takes some research because these sales figures are not public. Finding a sales volume can be as simple as walking into the grocery store and chatting with a produce or meat employee. An average grocery store will produce around $250,000 a week in sales. There are some that do $1 million+ in sales a week. In general, areas with strong performing stores are ripe for more competition because in theory there are more dollars in the market to transfer to the new store. Conversely if all the stores in the trade are poor performers then a new store will likely be a poor performer as well because the purchasing power is just not there to support it.

Gravitec Development also has an annual conference that focuses on store site selection. I attended this conference several times years ago and recently returned to it to speak about our Planned Grocery® platform. This has always been a relatively small conference. At this recent conference 85 people attended, along with 18 spouses. The recent conference started out with remarks from Mr. Puffer and then there was presentation on Aldi from Dr. David Rogers of DSR Marketing Systems. This presentation went over Aldi's strengths and weaknesses and he also went into details that pertained to the SITESPLUS model. Mr. Puffer then discussed the next SITESPLUS update formal release. Other presentations focused on beacon technology, using cell tower data to count customers, misleading maps and statistics, and the proliferation of small organic stores. During the writing of this book MTN Retail Advisors has taken over putting on this conference. As of 2017, this conference is now called the Gravisite Site-Selection Conference.

CHAPTER 15

Orbital Insight (Aerial Analytics)

Orbital Insight provides location analytics of satellite imagery. This process involves pulling data from images and comparing that data over time. In 2015, the company closed a $8.7 million Series A round led by Sequoia venture capital. Orbital Insight has developed machine learning programs to automate image classification. This technology can take a satellite image and count the number of cars in a parking lot for example. Why this is important to investors is that because the number of cars in a parking lot directly corresponds to a retailer's sales. A steady drop in cars could cause a retailer to miss its projected sales numbers. The Orbital Insight website claims that they have cataloged one million parking lot images, four trillion pixels, and 700 million cars across six years' worth of imagery.[1] Orbital Insight has this technology set up so that they can monitor and quantify retail traffic patterns in the parking lots of over 90 major retailers in the United States. This involves measuring over 100,000 parking lots. Car counts are statistically normalized daily by time of day to create mean observations for each retailer's portfolio of locations. From here this data can used to create short- and long-term trends.

Figure 15.1 shows 4 methods Orbital Insight uses to gather and analyze data: Data at Scale, Proprietary Algorithms, On-demand Platform, and Contextual Insights.

Orbital Insight also provides data on the global crude oil inventories by tracking over 20,000 storage tanks in 800+ tank farms around the world. Some of these locations are public record, but others are located and identified by Orbital Insights research. A propriety shadow-detection algorithm is used to continuously monitor global oil storage. An analysis

---

[1] https://orbitalinsight.com/solutions/us-retail-traffic-indices/

Data at Scale	Proprietary Algorithms	On-demand Platform	Contextual Insights
Diverse satellite, unmanned-aerial vehicle, and terrestrial data sources fuel your knowledge about Earth.	Innovations in computer vision and machine learning algorithms interpret imagery into insights.	Flexible and reliable historical, time-based, and location-based information.	Increased statistical sampling builds confidence levels and well-informed decisions.

Figure 15.1 Orbital Insight uses satellite imagery combined with proprietary algorithms

can then be generated to estimate individual tank volumes and reports can be run to aggregate the data into national, regional, and global oil supplies. By working with all of the major satellite providers Orbital Insight can measure crude oil volumes in regions where there this little or no data such as China, India, Nigeria, and Brazil.[2]

Another area that Orbital Insight is focusing on is monitoring the world water supply. As water is essential for humanity, many countries around the world are challenged with maintaining a steady supply of usable water. Orbital Insight monitors changes in the surface water reserves all over the world with bi-weekly scans. This data helps us understand the short- and long-term trends with these water bodies. By having data on these water bodies, government organizations can understand and plan better for the future.

As the most populous country in the world, China is a country that many organizations are trying to understand better. Orbital Insight has developed an economic index which does just that. Satellite Imagery is used to create data on over 30 major cities in China. Economic activity is measured in various ways by counting and studying the changing features in the satellite images. Building square footage is estimated using trigonometry by studying the shadows of the buildings. Oil storage, mentioned earlier, and the development of coal plants, wind farms, and solar energy farms can all be quantified. The import and export activity can be studied by looking at the port, rail, and airport activity.

---

[2] https://orbitalinsight.com/solutions/world-oil-storage-index/.

CHAPTER 16

Conclusion

Location analytics is driving decision making more and more every day. We see it all the time as more and more customers start using our Planned Grocery® platform or they take advantage of our streaming plan where we stream our Planned Grocery data directly into their existing mapping platform. Technology is transforming the way we shop, eat, and drive and this affects real estate in a big way. The companies, analysis methods, and data sources mentioned in this book are just some of the ways to better understand location analytics.

The big takeaway is that you need to understand that there are layers of spatial data. These layers may be proprietary to your organization, they may be free, they may come with your GIS software, or they many have an annual licensing fee. These layers can be easily shared through the organization and with the right software they can be analyzed to provide better location awareness to the organization. First you need to clearly define your organizations problems they are trying to solve. Then look for the data and analysis tools to get those results.

I am excited about the growth in the location analytics and data scientists' fields. I recently spoke with a data scientist who worked for a Wall Street investment company and thought to myself that I wished this job title had existed 25 years ago! In the computer mapping job field, you must be a data scientist first to know what data to use and what data not to use. You will be asked lots of questions about data that does not exist. So, you need to know what data is out there and what data you can create on your own. Location analytics is an exciting and growing field. If you find a job in this field, I hope that it challenges you and brings you as much joy as it has me over the years.

About the Author

David Z. Beitz is Partner and Co-Founder of Beitz and Daigh Geographics, a firm specializing in the use of Geographic Information Systems (GIS) primarily for the real estate business sector. Beitz's team also created Planned Grocery® a location analytics platform used by many grocery retailers, shopping center developers, and investment banks to track the development cycle of grocery stores across the United States. Having worked with shopping center owners, real estate investors, developers, brokers, investment banking professionals, and Internet entrepreneurs; Beitz has a diverse skill set in providing his clients with advanced location research and marketing as well as online mapping applications. Having developed innovative systems (some proprietary) for the use of GIS in Real Estate, he is always looking for new ways to help clients leverage spatial technology to their benefit.

Beitz graduated from the University of South Carolina with a Bachelor's Degree of Science from the College of Science and Mathematics and today has over 25 years of GIS experience (four years in Transportation Planning and 14 years in Real Estate, six years in GIS Consulting). He holds the Real Estate Development Certificate from the Urban Land Institute (2010), is a LEED Green Associate—Green Building Certification Institute (2009), and his various teams have received two Special Achievement Awards from ESRI (2001, 2012). Beitz has contributed to articles referencing GIS in Computerworld,[1] LBxJornal,[2] and GreenBiz.com.[3] Also data from the Planned Grocery® application that his team built has been mentioned in the *Wall Street Journal, Bloomberg, Business Insider,* and *Forbes.*

---

[1] Sandra Gittlen http://computerworld.com/article/2504009/business-intelligence/putting-the--where--into-your-analytics.html

[2] http://lbxjournal.com/articles/retail-leasing-agents/260326

[3] http://greenbiz.com/blog/2014/02/11/online-maps-speed-solar-site-selection

Index

OTHER TITLES IN OUR BIG DATA AND BUSINESS ANALYTICS COLLECTION

Mark Ferguson, University of South Carolina, Editor

- *Business Intelligence and Data Mining* by Anil Maheshwari
- *Data Mining Models* by David L. Olson
- *Big Data War: How to Survive Global Big Data Competition* by Patrick Park
- *Analytics Boot Camp: Basic Analytics for Business Students and Professionals* by Linda Herkenhoff and John Fogli

FORTHCOMING TITLES FOR THIS COLLECTION

- *Predictive Analytics: An Introduction to Big Data, Data Mining, and Text Mining* by Barry Keating
- *Business Analytics: A Data-Driven Decision Making Approach for Business* by Amar Sahay

Announcing the Business Expert Press Digital Library

Concise e-books business students need for classroom and research

This book can also be purchased in an e-book collection by your library as

- a one-time purchase,
- that is owned forever,
- allows for simultaneous readers,
- has no restrictions on printing, and
- can be downloaded as PDFs from within the library community.

Our digital library collections are a great solution to beat the rising cost of textbooks. E-books can be loaded into their course management systems or onto students' e-book readers.
The **Business Expert Press** digital libraries are very affordable, with no obligation to buy in future years. For more information, please visit **www.businessexpertpress.com/librarians**. To set up a trial in the United States, please email **sales@businessexpertpress.com**.

Lightning Source UK Ltd.
Milton Keynes UK
UKHW020821200222
398943UK00005B/318